TRAPUNTO

The Handbook of Stuffed Quilting

by Sue H. Rodgers

To Evelyn
Happy Quilting

Sue H. Rodgers

12/17/90

**MOON
OVER THE
MOUNTAIN**

PUBLISHING COMPANY

I would like to dedicate this book to my husband Bob and to my best friend, mentor, and quilting buddy Judy B. Dales. Thanks to both of you for moral support in this project and many others in the past.

Sue H. Rodgers

▲

Project Director: Bonnie Leman
Editor: Marie Shirer
Book Designer: Kathryn Wagar Wright
Illustrator: Marla Gibbs Stefanelli
Photographer: Jerry DeFelice

▲

Published by
Moon Over The Mountain Publishing Company
6700 West 44th Avenue, Wheatridge, Colorado 80033, U.S.A.
Library of Congress 90-063224
ISBN 0-943721-07-5

▲

Contents

▲

Made by the author, "American Heritage" (detail drawing on facing page) is in the collection of Elisabeth S. Rodgers.

An Introduction to Stuffed Quilting

Trapunto–or stuffed quilting– is an elegant finishing touch that makes a fine quilt spectacular by heightening the texture on the quilted surface. The sculptured look of trapunto is achieved by inserting extra stuffing into areas delineated by lines of fine quilting. These raised designs reflect the light and stand out from the background, giving a richness lacking in unstuffed quilts.

The trapunto tradition in the United States reached its zenith in the first third of the 19th century, and the lavish white-work quilts that survive from that era provide testimony to the stitching and artistic skill of the makers and inspiration for today's quilters. These opulent works represent what Dr. Robert Bishop, in his book *America's Quilts and Coverlets*, calls the quilter's "final test of craftsmanship . . . no needleworker started a white-work spread until she was sure of her patience and proficiency . . . draftsmanship and craftsmanship had to be exacting."

These great 19th-century American trapunto quilts were created in two steps. First a fine cotton top was quilted to a loosely woven backing to create elegant design areas. The areas were then stuffed with cotton, either by slitting the backing or by pulling apart the loose weave of the backing and inserting the filling with a broom straw. Channels were often filled by inserting candlewicking with a tapestry needle. Then a second backing of fine cotton (sometimes with batting, sometimes not) was added to hide the slits and tails of candlewicking, which were allowed to stick out of holes in the channels. Finally, close background quilting was done around the raised areas.

Modern quilters have, I feel, avoided trapunto because of the tedious techniques used by their ancestors and the feeling that these quilts were too fragile to be used. Almost everyone, myself included, admired the elegant old quilts with their beautiful embossed designs created by the stuffing and enhanced by dense background quilting, but we were discouraged by the process. By the mid-1970s, I discovered that my favorite part of quiltmaking was the hand quilting. Trapunto would allow me to concentrate on that aspect of quilting, eliminating the steps of piecing or appliquéing. When I saw the American Eagle pattern in 1976, I finally decided to try a trapunto quilt, as this was the pattern I had always wanted for my bed.

The making of "American Heritage" (detail drawing shown above) was truly a hands-on learning experience during which I used some traditional methods but also made some discoveries. To stuff the centers of the circles around the eagle, I painstakingly separated fibers and pushed polyester filling into the area with a toothpick. But, because of the large unquilted areas in the pattern, I decided to put batting in the quilt in the normal way, quilt it, and slip cording and stuffing between the backing and batting. This procedure worked beautifully, requiring less stuffing because just a bit of added filler pushed the batting up to give a full effect. Most importantly, the process eliminated the need for a second backing.

To fill the channels that delineated the eagle, I used a short tapestry needle to insert polyester cable cording, the same material that is used to make piping for pillows and upholstery. The short needle made this a time-consuming process. When I was ready to fill the rays around the eagle, I discovered a 6"-long weaving needle, which significantly speeded up the process of stuffing.

In the 12 years since "American Heritage" was completed, I have made a series of trapunto bed quilts and wall hangings, refining my quilting method and making other discoveries that have added to developing a fast, easy stuffing technique. The polyester cable cord has been replaced with soft, bulky acrylic yarn that gives a puffed effect without stiffness. I now use the 6" needle not only to fill channels, but also to stuff flower petals, leaves, and other irregularly shaped areas. Because there is no slitting–only small puncture holes from the needle–the quilts are reversible, durable, and functional. The backs of these quilts can be turned up for everyday use and the front sides for "company," allowing twice the use before the need for washing.

My love of raised quilting has only intensified in the intervening years, and I now incorporate trapunto in most of my quilts. The contrast between the high relief of stuffed areas that reflect light and the darker valleys along the quilting lines adds a wonderful sparkle and tactile allure to a quilt. These quilts want to be touched. I hope that the following techniques for creating trapunto quilts and projects will encourage you to try this exciting style.

Choosing a Design

Designs for trapunto quilts can be adapted from many sources. You don't have to be an artist to create a pattern. For inspiration, look at old quilts. Flowers, leaves, stems, feather circles, and fancy borders can all be stuffed. You can outline shapes with stuffed channels that are created with two parallel lines of quilting. Many applique patterns can be used for trapunto. I sometimes use cut-paper "snowflakes" for trapunto on quilts and clothing. (See pages 49-51 for patterns.) Just remember to create areas that are entirely enclosed so they can be filled. In the examples here, note the many ways that a single motif can be varied for trapunto.

The original flower, as seen in version 1, could be stuffed as given, providing the flower is not too big. Large areas, such as those in this design, can be stuffed, but they tend to lack definition. This version would be very soft and puffy. Versions 2 and 3 give more definition to the flower shape by adding parallel lines to create channels. These versions will have the effect of an outline drawing.

Examples 4, 5, and 6 all add lines to the flower to delineate the petals. By making smaller segments within the flower, the flower itself can be made much larger. All of these versions will have a soft, puffy effect, with version 6 slightly less so because the segments are smaller.

Versions 7 and 8 fill in the petals and leaves in different ways. Example 7 uses curved lines to create an outline effect on the petals, while the leaves are segmented and will be puffy when stuffed. In version 8, straight lines fill in the areas to create channels butted next to each other. When stuffed, the raised centers of the channels will catch the light, and the quilted lines will create darker areas to give a "washboard" effect. To me, this version is very graphic and modern. Version 9 combines several techniques of filling for interest and variety.

Several conclusions can be drawn from these examples. Parallel lines added to a

1-original flower   *2-outline*   *3-double outline*

4-segmented   *5-stencil segment*   *6-smaller segments with stencil look*

7-filling with curved lines   *8-filling with straight lines*   *9-combination*

pattern to create channels give the feeling of an outline drawing. Large stuffed areas will look softer than smaller stuffed areas, and channels butted next to each other give a dramatic light-and-dark effect.

Channels can be made in many widths, but I recommend a range of about ¼" to ¾". Those smaller than ¼" are difficult to stuff and those larger than ¾" require too many plies of yarn to look puffy. All the channels in the quilt "Square Dance" (shown on the back cover) are 1" wide, an exception to my general "rule." It required six plies of yarn and a lot of time to give this quilt a sculptured effect. In "Quasar" (shown on the inside front cover) the widest channel is ¾" with three plies of yarn, but the effect is still bold. Additional interest is created by combining various widths of channels and using crosshatched background quilting.

If you are intimidated by the idea of making a whole-cloth trapunto quilt, try adding stuffing as a decorative embellishment to a pieced or appliquéd quilt. Inspired by the fabulous 19th-century appliqué and trapunto quilts, I created

my quilt "Homage" (shown on page 26), which incorporates alternating chintz appliqué and large-scale piecing with trapunto borders. A contemporary setting for trapunto is "Snow Geese: The Fall Migration" (shown on page 27) in which trapunto "birds" (triangles filled with stuffed channels) fly over a layered-appliqué landscape to create a feeling of depth and to heighten the feeling of movement toward the upper right corner. In this quilt, a simple trapunto element adds great meaning.

Trapunto is also a wonderful embellishment for clothing. A single corded butterfly can transform a simple satin skirt into an elegant evening outfit. A group of different-sized butterflies enlivens an ordinary cotton skirt, or an inexpensive cotton chambray shirt is transformed into "dressy" sportswear. A trapunto vest in a neutral color or a collar with a single motif such as a flower or a snowflake can be an accessory to top almost any outfit. (See photos on pages 26 and 27.) A section on trapunto clothing and accessories with some specific techniques and ideas follows later in the book.

How To Do Trapunto

Fabrics for Trapunto

The traditional fabric for trapunto quilts was a loosely woven white cotton. I often use a 50 percent cotton/50 percent polyester fabric because the sheen of this decorator fabric accentuates the sculptured effect of trapunto. There are some polished fabrics available in quilt shops. Of course, muslin is suitable and now comes in widths up to 108". Whatever fabric you choose, the weave should be fairly loose. Inexpensive cotton muslin sheets are fine, but cotton percale sheets do not work well because the thread count is too dense to allow the needle holes to close up

after stuffing. I use the same fabric on both the top and back and, as you will note in "Square Dance" and "Quasar," I try to hide the seams in the design when possible to give the look of one large piece of cloth. All fabric should be washed and pressed before being used.

Exotic fabrics such as silks and satins are wonderful for clothing. When these are used they are backed with a loosely woven interfacing or cotton muslin, and no batting is used so that the garments will drape nicely. Further discussion follows in the section on clothing.

Marking the Quilt Top

Carefully mark your quilt top. Fabric-marking pencils made of chalk or a "non-photo" blue pencil will wash out of fabric, and the latter will keep a nice sharp point. The only disadvantages of the non-photo blue pencil are that you must press fairly hard to get a visible line and the fabric can move under the pencil. These pencils are made by several companies and can be purchased at art- or stationery-supply stores. If you choose to mark with a graphite pencil, use one of the "click-out" mechanical kind with a fine lead and make small, light dashes instead of solid lines. *Never use a hot iron on any marked lines, as this will set the marks in your fabric.*

You can transfer the designs by using stencils or templates, or by placing the pattern under a light-colored fabric and tracing. To help in seeing the pattern lines through fabric, place the pattern on a light box or tape it on a window or place it over a glass-top table with a lamp underneath.

Basting the Quilt

The layers of a trapunto quilt should be basted in much the same manner as any quilt. Since I quilt in a hoop, I always baste thoroughly as follows.

Wash and press the quilt backing and spread it out on a flat surface. If you are working on a small project or if you are lucky enough to have a large, hard surface for basting, tape the backing to this surface with masking tape to eliminate wrinkles. Smooth the batting over the backing, and then add the marked quilt top over the batting. If you have not been able to tape the backing to the surface, put some weight on the center of the quilt and gently pull on the backing to eliminate wrinkles. The first line of basting should be lengthwise down the center of the quilt. Stitch from the center to one end and then from the center to the other end. The second line of basting is from side to side through the center. *Never baste from corner to corner as this immediately distorts the quilt on the bias.* Now, working in each quarter of the quilt, baste lengthwise and crosswise to form a 6" grid. Before basting each quarter, put weight on the quilt and gently pull on the backing to eliminate wrinkles. When all four quarters are basted, trim away any excess batting, turn the edges of the backing over the top, and baste in place to protect the edges of the batting during the quilting process.

A neat trick is to use a plastic spoon to catch the point of the basting needle as it comes up through the quilt. This eliminates the troublesome needle-under-the-fingernail syndrome and really speeds the basting process.

Quilting Techniques

Because a certain amount of stress will be put on quilting lines during the stuffing process, these lines must be very firm or they will pull loose. Drawing from many sources, I have developed starting and stopping techniques that are very secure, yet use no visible knots or backstitches. All the starting, stopping, and crossing over are done between the top fabric and the batting so that when you stuff the quilt from the back, the threads will not be caught in the stuffing yarn. As with any quilt, you will start quilting in the center and work toward the edges. I suggest that you read through these quilting instructions entirely before starting a project.

Starting on a straight line

1 Thread the needle with a single strand of thread that is no more than 18" long. I prefer 100 percent cotton quilting thread over cotton-covered polyester because it is stronger and tangles less. For trapunto, it is traditional to match the color of the thread to that of the fabric being quilted. Tie a simple knot, leaving a 1½" to 1¾" tail behind the knot. Always tie the knot in the end that was closest to the spool, as this helps prevent shredding or breaking caused by pulling the thread through the fabric against the grain of the thread.

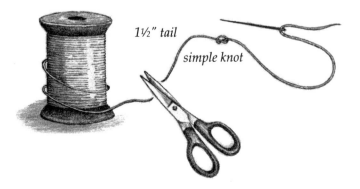

1½" tail
simple knot

2 Insert the needle into the line to be quilted 1" ahead of the spot where the first stitch is to begin.

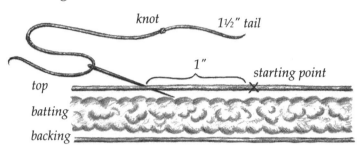

knot   1½" tail

top

batting

backing

1"   starting point

3 Keeping the needle between the top fabric and the batting, bring the point of the needle up at the starting point and pull the needle out of the top fabric.

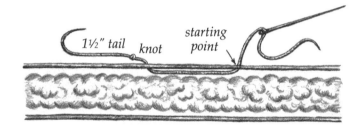

1½" tail   knot   starting point

4 Pop the knot down through the top fabric, and pull it between the fabric and batting until it stops just short of where the thread emerges, leaving a ½" tail hanging out and 1" of thread under the line to be quilted.

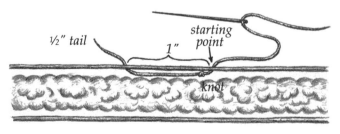

½" tail   1"   starting point   knot

5 Make the first stitch by inserting the needle slightly ahead of where the thread emerges from the quilt and, if possible, pierce the knot to lock the thread. This first stitch will appear on the top side of the quilt.

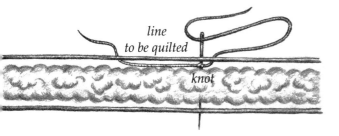

line to be quilted

knot

6 Take three or four more stitches. Pull the needle out of the quilt and gently tighten this first group of stitches. With the point of your needle pull the tail inside the quilt sandwich, or clip it. Note that you have quilted over the buried thread with these first stitches for a very secure start. Continue quilting, making groups of three or four stitches, pulling the needle out of the quilt, and gently tightening each group.

Starting on a curved line

To start on a curved line, proceed as above, but align the needle with the curve so that a maximum amount of thread will be under the line to be quilted.

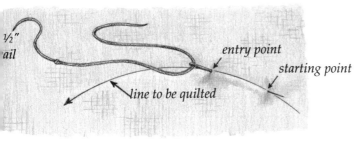

½" tail

entry point

starting point

line to be quilted

Finishing a line of quilting

My method of finishing a quilting line uses no knots or backstitches. Instead, you will make a "U turn" around the line of quilting between the top and the batting. To make the "U turn":

1 Always leave at least 4" of thread to finish a quilting line. Insert the needle into the top fabric only, as if to take a final stitch. Reversing

direction, keep the needle between the top fabric and the batting and run it along one side of the line of quilting for four or five stitches. Bring the point up next to a gap between two stitches in the line of quilting.

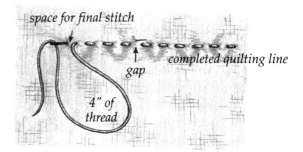

space for final stitch

completed quilting line

gap

4" of thread

2 Pull the needle through, but not all the way out of the fabric, at the same time pivoting the eye of the needle *counterclockwise* and keeping the needle flat against the quilt. When the needle reaches a right angle with the line of quilting, you will feel the eye "pop" into the gap between two stitches.

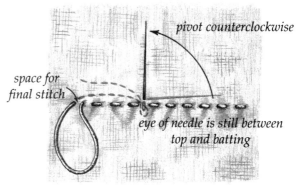

pivot counterclockwise

space for final stitch

eye of needle is still between top and batting

3 Still keeping the eye of the needle between the top fabric and the batting, push it through the gap in the quilting, pivot it *clockwise*, and push it back down the opposite side of the line of quilting. Use a thimble to protect your finger from the point of the needle if necessary.

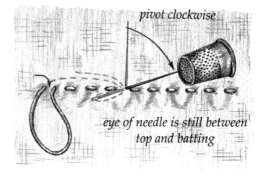

pivot clockwise

eye of needle is still between top and batting

4 Push the eye of the needle through the top fabric.

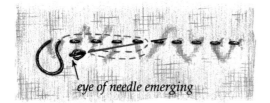

eye of needle emerging

5 Pull the needle out and clip and bury the thread. The thread has now made a "U turn" around the line of quilting between the top and the batting.

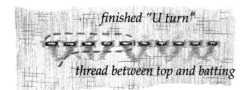

finished "U turn"

thread between top and batting

Continuing a straight or curved line

Sometimes you will run out of thread before a line of quilting is complete. This is often true when quilting a long line for one side of a channel. When continuing a line with a new thread, it is important to achieve evenly spaced quilting stitches on both the top and back of the quilt. To do this:

1 Finish the line with available thread as outlined above.

2 Insert the needle with the new thread 1" ahead of the point where the last stitch of the completed quilting went down into the top fabric, and bring the point of the needle up into the hole made by this last stitch.

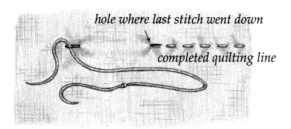

hole where last stitch went down

completed quilting line

3 Pop the knot through the fabric and pull it just up to the hole. Put the point of the needle back into the hole, through the knot if possible, and through the three layers.

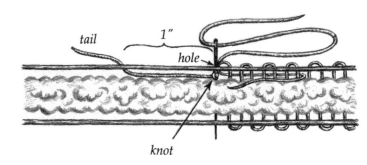

tail *1"* *hole*

knot

Make the first visible stitch on the back of the quilt to start a continuous, evenly spaced quilting line on both sides of the quilt.

Crossing over

1 You may "cross over" or "travel" when you still have thread on your needle and wish to move to a new line to quilt without finishing the previous line. Crossing over helps speed up the quilting by eliminating stopping and starting. At the end of quilting line A, cross over to line B between the top fabric and the batting. At the end of quilting line B cross over to line C, and so on.

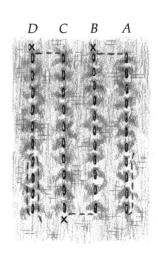

D   C   B   A

2 Take a tiny backstitch before continuing after a crossover (at each x in the figure above) to stabilize the previous line of quilting.

3 Be very careful to keep the crossovers between the top fabric and the batting when crossing over an area that is to be stuffed.

Stuffing Techniques

When all the quilting is finished, remove the basting and markings as necessary. Completely finish the edges of the quilt and wash it before stuffing. For your first attempts at stuffing, place the quilt in a hoop, back side up. This will help keep the quilt surface smooth and prevent pulling gathers along the channels as you stuff. Later, when you discover how much stuffing is enough, you will not need to use the hoop.

Ideally, all the stuffing is done with a 6"-long weaving or trapunto needle with a blunt point and an eye the size of that on a tapestry needle. Soft-sculpture or doll-making needles with sharp points do not work well because the point will pierce the threads of the fabric and tear holes. A tapestry needle may be used, but the longer needle is wonderful because it is so easy to grip when pulling the yarn into the quilt.

My favorite stuffing material is bulky acrylic yarn of the type used to wrap gift packages or tie little girls' pony tails. This yarn is soft but does not stretch as it is inserted into the quilt. You can use knitting or heavy rug yarn, but you should untwist the plies to eliminate the kink and stretch. The best fiber for stuffing yarn is acrylic or polyester, both of which are lightweight and washable. White or off-white are both fine for all quilts except those with very dark backings, in which case it is preferable to match the yarn to the color of the back so that no fibers of yarn show in the holes. A source list for these items is given on page 20.

Stuffing straight channels

1 Cut the yarn into 12" lengths. Do not try to use longer pieces of yarn, as they will pull apart as you insert them in the quilt. If using bulky acrylic yarn, divide each piece into three plies so that one ply can be used. If using heavy knitting or rug yarn, untwist the plies to eliminate the kinks and elasticity. You may need to make a

sample to determine how many plies of knitting or rug yarn will be needed to fill the channel or area to be stuffed.

2 Thread the needle in the same way you would a tapestry needle, having one long tail and one short tail.

3 Insert the needle into the backing fabric and, keeping the needle between the backing and batting, run it about 4" along the channel. With your hand underneath the hoop, push up on the needle in the channel and, at the same time, push the point back out through the backing. Pull and gently twist (do not yank) the eye of the needle into the channel. The eye of the needle is actually separating the threads of the fabric to form the hole. If using a short tapestry needle, you can gently push the eye of the needle into the channel with a fingernail, scoot the needle along about 4", and then push against the eye inside the channel to make the point emerge. Pull the yarn until the

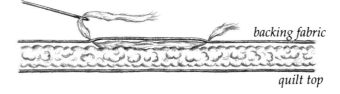

backing fabric

quilt top

tail just disappears into the channel. Grasp the point of the needle and pull the needle out of the quilt, continuing until the tail of the yarn just disappears into the channel.

4 Put a little tension on the yarn and clip. The yarn will pop back into the hole.

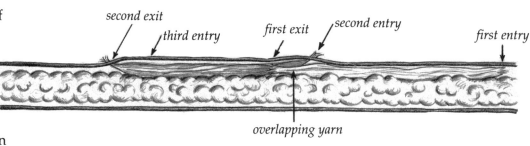

5 Place the point of the needle about ½" behind this exit hole and repeat the process so that the yarn will overlap to completely fill the channel. Clip the yarn again as in step 4.

second exit *third entry* *first exit* *second entry* *first entry*

overlapping yarn

6 Continue stuffing, overlapping and clipping each time until the channel is full. I prefer this overlapping method to the traditional way of re-entering the same hole because, although there are more holes, they are very small and will close. When you re-enter the same hole, the yarn can stretch or even tear the hole. Note: Please don't be tempted to scoot the long needle inside the channel as the yarn will probably break. After years of practice, I have found it is best to work in about 4" increments, whatever size needle is used.

Stuffing wider channels

1 For channels wider than about ¼", pull the yarn up in the needle so that you will be working with two tails of the same length.

2 For a ½" channel, put two plies in at a time, overlapping just as you did for the ¼" channel.

3 For a ¾" channel, put two plies along one edge of the channel, overlapping each segment. Then go back in and add another ply along the opposite edge of the channel, parallel to the first two plies, also overlapping each segment.

Stuffing curved channels

Curved channels are filled in the same manner as straight channels, but you only run the needle as far as the curve of the channels will allow without tearing the entry hole. For instance, if you are stuffing a channel around a 4" circle, you will probably not be able to run the needle more than 2" in the channel. Overlap the yarn in a curved channel the same way as in a straight channel, beginning each new segment of yarn ¼" behind the previous exit hole.

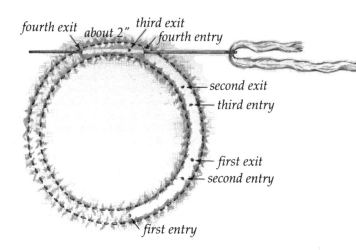

fourth exit *about 2"* *third exit* *fourth entry* *second exit* *third entry* *first exit* *second entry* *first entry*

Stuffing larger areas

1 Irregularly shaped areas are stuffed in the same way as channels, but usually without overlapping.

2 Thread the needle and pull the yarn up so that you will be working with two plies of the same length, as shown previously.

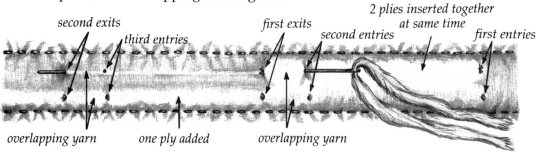

second exits *third entries* *first exits* *second entries* *2 plies inserted together at same time* *first entries*

overlapping yarn *one ply added* *overlapping yarn*

3 Put the needle into the area to be stuffed across the longest dimension, *always keeping the needle between the backing and batting.*

area to be stuffed

4 Pull the yarn into the area as you did for the channel, clip it, and bury the end.

5 Now insert the needle back into one of the holes and use it as a tool to move the yarn to one side of the area.

2 plies

6 Repeat these steps as outlined above using the same two holes. This time move the yarn to the opposite side of the area.

4 plies

7 Continue stuffing the area, alternating sides until the area is full but not hard. If you could see inside the quilt, the area would resemble this.

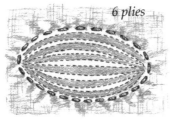

6 plies

8 To stuff areas with one narrow and one wide end, such as the teardrop shapes of a feather circle design, thread the needle with one ply slightly longer than the other. Insert the needle

across the area and pull the yarn inside, leaving one ply in the narrow end and two plies in the wide end.

How much is enough?

It does not take as much as one might think to stuff a channel or area because the yarn pushes the batting into the space; this makes the area appear to be full on the top side of the quilt. Fairly large spaces can be stuffed without problems of shifting because the sharp points of the batting (the same points that "beard") catch the yarn and hold it in place.

Just remember that it is much easier to put yarn in than to take it out. Yarn can be removed with a very small crochet hook, but it is tedious. Just keep checking the effect of the stuffing on the top side of the quilt as you work. If you begin to see gathers around a quilting line, you have overstuffed. My rule of thumb is one ply of bulky acrylic yarn for each ¼" of width in a channel or area, but as an area gets larger it may require more stuffing to achieve a sculptured effect. For example, the channels in "Square Dance" (shown on the back cover) are 1" wide and have six plies of yarn. If you are using untwisted knitting or rug yarn, make a sample to determine how much yarn is needed to fill the space. Then you can thread the needle with several strands at a time and/or pull the yarn tails even for the most efficient stuffing.

After you have the feeling for how much yarn is enough, you don't have to stuff the quilt in a hoop. When working on a bed quilt, I often spread it on a table. You can check to see whether a channel or area is sufficiently stuffed by holding the quilt up to the light.

Well, that's it! No slitting, no broom straws or toothpicks, and no second backing. With practice, you will find that this method of stuffing is much faster than the traditional way. And, even though there are more holes from overlapping, they are very small and with washing become almost invisible. Your finished product will be reversible to give you twice the wear and twice the enjoyment.

Trapunto on Bed Quilts

When designing a whole-cloth trapunto bed quilt, I do not make a full-size paper pattern for the entire quilt, as this would be unnecessary and difficult to handle. Instead, I begin by making a scale drawing of the quilt layout on graph paper, allowing 4" to 5" in both dimensions for shrinkage during the quilting and stuffing. Then, individual design elements are drafted full size. For instance, for the quilt "Blizzard of '83" (shown on inside back cover), I drew the window dividers directly onto the fabric with a pencil and yardstick, using my drawing as a guide for measurements. The individual snowflakes were then drafted and placed under the fabric and traced. This quilt is an example of a design where I hid the center seam in the design to create the illusion of one large piece of fabric.

I also make scale drawings of pieced and appliquéd bed quilts on which I plan to use trapunto embellishments. Then I design each trapunto element to fit a specific space, taking my measurements and shapes from this drawing. A good example of this design method is the quilt "Homage." All the designs for the trapunto were created to fit the specific needs of the quilt. However, the border design could be adapted to other sizes, as it is made up of a simple repeated unit. This border and the designs for the corner blocks are given in the project section with suggestions of how to adapt them for other quilts.

Trapunto on Clothing

Clothing is a wonderful place to use trapunto and a good place to try design ideas and techniques on a small-scale project. In this section, I would like to share some special pointers and design techniques that I use for making garments.

Fabrics, fillers, and backings

The same fabrics that were recommended for a trapunto quilt or wall hanging are appropriate for trapunto clothing also. I particularly like fabrics with a sheen, which emphasizes the relief of the stuffing. For clothing, more exotic fabrics such as silk, satin, or synthetics also can be used. Cottons and cotton blends should be washed before using.

The style and function of a garment will determine whether batting or other filler will be used. For a jacket, vest, or accessory that should be warm and doesn't need to drape or hang softly, it is appropriate to use batting or flannel between the top and backing. In this case the garment will be treated just like a large quilt. The design will be marked, the "quilt sandwich" layered, basted, finished around the edges, and washed. Finally the stuffing will be inserted into the underside of the piece as described earlier. Since the garment will be reversible, the same fabric should be used on both the top and back. You might even choose to use a different color on each side for variety. For lightweight clothing made of silk, satin, or other soft fabrics that you want to drape, hang nicely, or be cool, the batting should be eliminated. For these projects, the backing should be the same weight as the top fabric. For silks and satins, a loosely woven synthetic inner lining works well; for cottons such as a work shirt, a lightweight muslin or batiste is appropriate. The quilting and stuffing techniques are exactly the same as in a large quilt with one exception: *When quilting, you may not cross over an area to be corded or stuffed.* Without the batting acting as a buffer, these crossover threads would be caught and pulled during the stuffing process. *You may cross between areas, but not over!*

Embellishing ready-made garments

Ready-made shirts are fun and easy to embellish. Choose a shirt with a flat, unpleated back. Wash and iron the shirt and mark the design on the outside. Insert a piece of muslin inside and handstitch it to the seams around the shoulders and the armholes. The bottom edge is left loose so

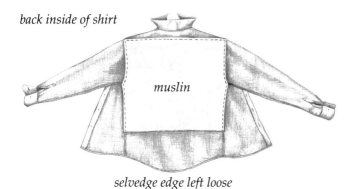

back inside of shirt

muslin

selvedge edge left loose

that no hemstitches show through to the outside. The quilting and stuffing are then done as in any trapunto project, but without crossing over any area to be stuffed. For added interest, you can use pearl cotton or metallic threads for the quilting.

Other ready-made garments, such as skirts, can be decorated in the same manner simply by adding a backing, stitching, and stuffing. It is not always necessary to back the whole garment. For instance, for a border around the bottom of a skirt, you could just add a wide facing

around the hem. I recommend that the purchased garment be washed or dry-cleaned before quilting is added.

Constructing trapunto garments from patterns

If you are constructing a garment to embellish with trapunto, choose a pattern *one size larger* than you would normally use to allow for shrinkage during the quilting and stuffing process. Also, in order to quilt in a hoop, do not cut out and construct the garment before quilting. Instead, using tracing paper, copy the outline of the commercial pattern, making a complete shape wherever the directions indicate to "place on fold." Add the designs for trapunto and background quilting, and ink the new pattern with an opaque marking pen. Now lay the fabric over these patterns and trace the outline and the embellishments, leaving enough room between each piece for cutting when the quilting is completed.

The garment is layered, basted, and quilted in the usual manner, except that the quilting is stopped a minimum of 1" away from any points of construction such as shoulder and underarm seams, and thread is left hanging to finish the quilting after the garment is constructed.

After all the quilting and construction are complete, the garment is washed by hand in mild soap and rolled in a towel to remove the water. It is either dried flat on a towel or on a plastic hanger after being "blocked" or pulled gently into shape by matching bottom edges and armholes.

Some simple design tricks

When designing embellishments for trapunto clothing, I often work with one shape in various sizes. A motif such as a butterfly can be enlarged and reduced on a copying machine, then filled in various ways. I make lots of copies, cut them out, then play with them on the garment pattern until a pleasing effect is obtained. Try this with some of the patterns (given later in the book) such as the flowers and butterflies. It is fun and easy, even for the novice designer. If the size of a pattern is enlarged or reduced, the width of the channels may need to be adjusted.

It is also fun to make design elements flow continuously over a garment. To do this, lay your commercial pattern out on a flat surface, fold under the seam allowances, and butt the pattern pieces next to each other along the seam line. Lay a large piece of tracing paper over the patterns, and draw the design or play with individual elements so that they go over the seams. If your vest pattern has straight side seams, they can be eliminated by overlapping the pattern pieces and cutting the vest or jacket in one continuous piece. Then the only seams that will need to butt are the shoulder seams.

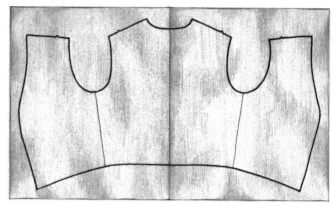

*side seams eliminated
on a vest pattern*

Trapunto Accessories
for Clothing and the Home

Clothing and household accessories are wonderful items to embellish with trapunto; they give an opportunity to try this technique on a small scale. In the project section you will find instructions for a collar, two purses, a belt, and a pillow. Additional ideas can be found in the craft and home-decorating sections of commercial pattern catalogs. A trapunto motif may be added to the pocket or front of an apron, the side of a tote bag, or the corner or edge of place mats and a table runner. Holiday items such as stockings or tree skirts may include trapunto.

Trapunto pillows are a beautiful addition to any home, and there are directions for many styles, shapes, and sizes of pillows in pattern catalogs. Mark and quilt the pillow top; then construct the pillow, making the cover so that it fits snugly over a firm pillow form. Put a zipper or Velcro on the back so that the cover may be washed. Finally, stuff the trapunto and insert the pillow form.

A trapunto design may be added to the top of a fabric-covered box. Mark, quilt, wash, and stuff the design before incorporating it on the box top.

Designs for trapunto accessories

Any of the patterns for flowers, butterflies, feather borders, or snowflakes found in the project section are appropriate for accessories. In addition to these, a fun and easy method of creating your own original motifs is by paper cutting. Snowflakes can be produced by folding a square of paper into six segments and cutting into the folds and edges. Other effects can be achieved by folding the square into eight segments. Symmetrical patterns such as hearts, flowers, stars, or simple butterflies can be created by folding a piece of paper in half and cutting half the desired shape on the folded edge. Actually, the butterfly pattern in the purse project could be cut in this manner. You can also layer several pieces of paper and "multiple cut" designs for quilting patterns that repeat. Experiment with paper cutting; there are several good books listed in the bibliography that will help you to create a large variety of designs. Just remember to make designs for enclosed areas that can be stuffed. If you cut your paper patterns from freezer paper, an added benefit is that they may be bonded directly to the fabric as a quilting guide. This eliminates the need for marking with a pencil on fabrics that can't be washed such as silks and satins, and it is also a convenient way to work on dark fabrics.

To bond a freezer-paper pattern, place the shiny side down on the right side of the fabric, and press with the hottest setting appropriate for the fabric without steam. Work on a hard surface covered with a dish towel rather than a padded ironing board. You may now quilt around the pattern near the edges of the paper. To remove a bonded pattern, lightly warm it and lift it from the fabric.

Caring for Trapunto

Trapunto quilts and garments are cared for in exactly the same way as other quilts. If the fabric is washable, a garment may be carefully washed with mild soap and warm water on a gentle cycle and dried flat or on a hanger. I do not machine dry these garments, as the tumbling action is very abrasive, and they lose their shape.

Bed quilts may be washed in the machine by filling the tub with warm water and mild soap, and immersing the quilt to soak, without agitation. After about 30 minutes, the quilt is spun, the tub is refilled with warm water, and the quilt is spun again to rinse it. *Never agitate the quilt*, as this breaks the quilting threads. The rinse-and-spin steps are repeated until all the soap is removed and a final hard spin removes as much of the water as possible. Dry the quilt over two clotheslines to avoid stress on the quilting stitches. If you do not have long clotheslines, spread a piece of plastic (a new painting drop cloth is perfect) on your bed, and dry the quilt flat, turning it over one time.

For clothing made of fabric that requires dry-cleaning, request that the cleaners press the garment by hand around the trapunto areas to avoid flattening them. Most cleaners will honor this request if you point out that the garment is handmade and needs special care.

▲　▲　▲　▲　▲　▲　▲

Well, I hope that this section of the book has helped teach you "everything you've wanted to know" about trapunto. At least, I hope that I have taken the mystery out of the subject so that you can begin to experiment with this vibrant style of quilting, which may have seemed too unfamiliar, difficult, and time-consuming in the past. I expect that once you have tried some of the small projects in this book using my streamlined stuffing method, you will want to incorporate trapunto in many of your quilts and perhaps even create a large white-work bed quilt. You will probably find, as I have, that you are no longer satisfied with the flat look of an unstuffed feather circle or fancy border. Trapunto gives such areas greater definition and clarity and makes a quilt shimmer with reflected light. To this day, when I walk through a quilt show and see an unstuffed white-work quilt or a fancy quilting design in a pieced or appliqued quilt, my fingers get itchy! When asked, "Why bother to stuff your quilts? It's so much extra work," my answer is easy: "Because they will have more pizzazz and will look more vibrant and alive. My fast, easy method of stuffing is not so hard to do; it's worth the extra time!" I hope you agree that trapunto is a glorious finishing touch that is worth the effort and that you will have fun stuffing your quilts for many years to come. Now on to the projects.

Tools, materials, and resources for projects

In addition to the usual quilting and sewing supplies, the following tools and materials will be used in many of the projects. They may be found in stationery or art stores, quilt shops, or even at the grocery store!

▲ A 6"-long blunt-point needle, available in quilt shops or from Quilts & Other Comforts, Box 394, Wheatridge, CO 80034-0394.

▲ Bulky acrylic yarn. This yarn can be found in some card shops and craft stores, at quilt shops, or by mail from Quilts & Other Comforts.

▲ Tracing paper. This comes in pads of various sizes or rolls of various lengths and widths. This paper is used for making patterns.

▲ A Salem, C-Thru, or Quilter's ruler. These are all clear plastic and are very helpful and convenient for tracing patterns. C-Thru rulers come in many shapes and sizes and can be found in stationery and art-supply stores.

▲ Masking tape

▲ A black Sharpie permanent marker made by Sanford. The ink in these pens is very opaque and perfect for pattern making. They can be found in the grocery store, or stationery or art stores.

▲ Non-photo blue colored pencil or click-out (mechanical) graphite pencil for transferring patterns to fabric.

▲ Sharp-pointed paper scissors

▲ Stapler

▲ Freezer paper. This may be found in the food-wrap section of the grocery store or at restaurant-supply stores.

Dove Wall Hanging

A photo of the Dove wall hanging is on page 28. Patterns may be found on pages 38 and 39. The pattern for the Dove wall hanging is 18½" square. After quilting and stuffing (which cause a quilt to shrink in size), it will finish about 18¼". If you add the optional hanging loops, the wall hanging will end up about 19¾" high. The pattern may be executed in two ways. Version 1 has the areas around the bird cut out. Version 2 is a whole-cloth quilt (without cutout areas), and is less difficult to make. *Read all instructions and study pattern before beginning either of the versions.*

Materials

1. Two 26" squares and one 1¾" x 25" strip of white, off-white, or light-colored fabric
2. One 25" square of batting
3. Sewing and quilting thread to match fabric
4. "Fray Check™," "No Fray™," or Elmer's Glue
5. Fabric-marking pencil and a black felt-tip pen
6. Stuffing yarn and stuffing needle
7. Curtain rod or wood dowel for hanging
8. A 24" square of tracing paper
9. 14" quilting hoop (optional)

Tracing the pattern

1 Tape the piece of tracing paper over the partial pattern in the book, matching center of paper with center of the dove design.

2 Using a black felt-tip pen, trace all the lines of the bird and frame, including those marked "hemline," "outside hemline," the lines of flowers A, B1, and C, and dots 1-7. It is not necessary to mark the Xs or the arrow on flower B1.

3 Lift the paper, turn it a quarter turn, realign the center square, and trace flowers A, B1, and C and lines X, Y, and "outside hemline" a second time.

4 Lift the paper, and repeat step 3 twice more so that there are flowers and lines on all four sides of the bird.

5 Extend lines Y, lines Z, and the "outside hemlines" to complete the corners of the frame as shown in the diagram at left.

6 Trace flower B2 in each corner, centering it on the space and positioning it with the small arrow pointing to the corner of the inside square. When finished, your completed paper pattern should look like the quilt diagram.

Preparing for quilting

1 Center one of the 26" square pieces of fabric over the pattern, right side up, and tape it in place. Trace all lines, and mark dots 1-7.

2 Smooth the other 26" square of fabric, wrong side up, on a flat surface, and center the batting and the marked top over the back. Baste the layers.

Version 1: with cutout areas

1 Using the pattern as a guide, quilt all lines except those marked "hemline." Stop quilting at dots 1-7, leaving thread to finish quilting after the hemming is finished.

2 Starting with "cutout area 1," cut ¼" outside of "hemlines" around the bird and inside the frame.

3 Using the head of a straight pin, put a small dot of "Fray Check," "No Fray," or Elmer's Glue on both the top and back at points where clips will go into deep angles.

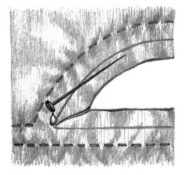

4 Turn a ¼" hem to inside, clipping where necessary on curves and deep angles. Pin and blindstitch. If necessary, take several whipstitches in deep clips.

5 Repeat steps 2-4 for cutout areas 2 through 5.

6 Finish off quilting lines with leftover thread and add short lines of quilting where the tail, wings, and chest touch the frame.

Version 2: whole cloth

Quilt all the lines of the dove and frame, including the lines of the bird and those inside the square marked "hemline." Disregard dots 1-7. *Do not quilt the line called "outside hemline."*

Finishing (either version)

1 To make the hanging loops (optional): Fold the 1¾"-wide strip of fabric in half lengthwise, right sides together. Pin and stitch ¼" from the raw edges. Turn the tube and press. Cut five 4"-long pieces from this strip for the hanging loops. Fold each in half and pin.

2 Cut ¼" from "outside hemline" of the quilt.

3 Evenly space and insert the hanging loops between the layers of fabric across the top of the quilt.

4 On all four sides, turn a ¼" hem to the inside on both the top and backing; pin.

5 Blindstitch the backing to the quilt top on each side, catching the hanging loops as you stitch across the top.

6 Wash the quilt gently by hand and roll it in a towel to remove the water. Block the wall hanging to a square shape by gently pulling the corners and dry it flat on a towel.

7 Stuff the channels and areas indicated on the pattern with an X, according to the general instructions.

8 Hang the quilt on a curtain rod or wooden dowel.

Flower Garden Vest

A photograph of the vest is on page 26; patterns are on pages 40-41.

Materials

1. A commercial hip- or waist-length vest pattern with only two basic pattern pieces, one size larger than your normal size
2. Two one-yard pieces of fabric (or two pieces long enough for your pattern)
3. One piece of batting 36" x 45", or enough batting for your pattern
4. Sewing and quilting thread to match
5. Fabric-marking pencil and a black felt-tip pen
6. 14" quilting hoop (optional)
7. Stuffing yarn and stuffing needle
8. One 36" x 45" piece of tracing paper, or enough to create your pattern, plus several pieces of 8½" x 11" tracing paper

Making the pattern

1 Press the back and front pieces of the vest pattern. To make a complete pattern for vest back, fold tracing paper in half and place this fold on center back of pattern. Trace dashed seam lines, then reverse paper and mark other half. Unfold pattern. At the shoulder and underarm, draw lines ⅝" outside these lines. At the armholes, neck, and bottom draw lines ¼" inside these lines.

2 Trace the vest front pattern in the same manner, drawing on the dashed lines and adding ⅝" outside the lines at shoulder and side. Add lines ¼" inside the lines at the armhole, neck, front, and bottom.

3 Using a pencil, draw three parallel lines on the front pattern, one 6", one 5¾", and one 5½" from the bottom and front edges. Also draw three parallel channel lines on the back pattern

piece, one 6", one 5¾", and one 5½" from the bottom edge. The front and back patterns now have a 5½"-wide border in which you can arrange the flower motifs as diagramed below.

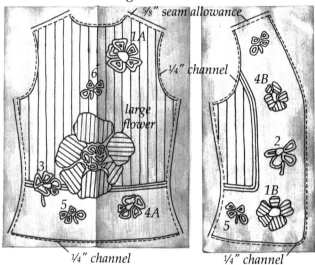

4 Center the vest back pattern. Place the fold over the dashed line on the pattern for the large flower, letting the bottom petals overlap the channel lines by about ¾". Trace with a pen.

5 On one of the small pieces of tracing paper trace flowers 1A, 1B, 4A, and 4B. On another piece trace the remaining small flowers. Make several photocopies of these sheets. Cut the flowers apart, and play with them on the vest patterns, referring to the diagram above. Depending on the length of your pattern and your garment size, you may or may not be able to copy my vest pattern exactly. The diagram given is for a size 14. When you have an arrangement you like, mark the position of each flower, then slip it under the tracing paper and trace each one with an ink pen.

6 Ink the three channel lines and erase any unnecessary pencil lines.

7 Finally, working outward from the center back, add vertical parallel lines 1" apart for the background quilting.

Transferring the pattern to the fabric

1 Center one of the pieces of fabric right side up over the the back pattern and trace all the lines.

2 Put the same piece of fabric over the front pattern so that the armhole hooks around the armhole of the back as shown below. Trace all the lines.

3 To reverse the front, turn pattern over, then trace again. Leave enough room between the pattern pieces to cut them out (but do not cut pieces apart yet), and allow enough extra fabric around the edges to use a quilting hoop. Note: This layout works for a size 14. If your vest is larger, you may only be able to fit the back and one front together and will need extra fabric for the second front. *Be sure to reverse the second front by turning the paper pattern over before tracing.*

Quilting the vest

1 Smooth the vest lining wrong side up on a table, put the batting and marked top over it, and baste.

2 Quilt all the lines, stopping 2" away from the shoulder and side seam lines, and leaving a 6" tail of thread to finish the quilting later.

Constructing the vest

1 Cut ¼" away from the outside line of the armholes, neck, front opening, and bottom. Cut on the lines that are ⅝" away from the lines marking the shoulder and underarm seams.

2 Pin the shoulder and side seams of the top piece of fabric, right sides together. Be sure to match the channel lines at the side seams. Fold the lining and batting out of the way and stitch these seams. Press seam allowances open.

3 Trim the batting so that the edges just butt together over the seams.

4 Turn the ⅝" seam allowances of the back lining to the inside and blindstitch them together over the top seam at the shoulders and sides.

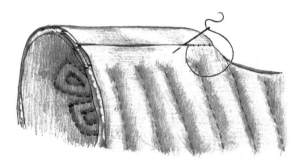

Finishing the vest

1 Finish the quilting lines with the leftover tails of thread.

2 Around the armholes, neck, front opening, and bottom, turn a ¼" hem to the inside on both the top and backing and blindstitch the folded edges together.

3 Wash the vest by hand, rolling it in a towel to remove the water, and block it to shape by gently pulling the bottoms even. Dry the vest flat on a towel or on a plastic hanger.

4 Stuff the ½" channels of the large flower with two plies of yarn, the narrow channels with one ply, and the areas marked with an X as necessary, according to the general instructions.

Left, ruffled "Trellis" pillow
▲ *Instructions for the pillow are on pages 34-36.*

Below, "White on White," 80" x 106"
Made by the author, this quilt is in the collection of Jean Gascoigne.
▲ *Patterns for the flowers are on pages 40, 41, and 44.*

Left, "Flower Garden" vest
▲ *Instructions for the vest are on pages 23 and 24.*

Below, "Homage," 79" x 98"
▲ *Patterns for the feather quilting motifs are on pages 37, 46, and 47.*

Above, "Snow Geese: the Fall Migration,"
43" x 43"

Right, trapunto collar
▲ *Instructions for the collar are on pages 29 and 30.*

Below, trapunto belt
▲ *Instructions for the belt are on page 33.*

Left, "Dove" wall hanging, 18$^{1}/_{4}$" x 19$^{1}/_{4}$"
▲ Instructions for two versions of the wall hanging are on pages 21 and 22.

Below, trapunto purses ▲ Instructions for both purses are on pages 30-32.

28

Trapunto Collar

A photograph of the collar is on page 27; patterns are on pages 42-44.

Materials

1. Two pieces of fabric 27" long by 31" wide
2. One piece of batting 27" x 31"
3. Sewing and quilting thread to match
4. Hook and eye
5. Stuffing yarn and needle
6. 24" x 32" piece of tracing paper for pattern
7. Fabric-marking pencil and a black felt-tip pen

Making your pattern

1 Fold tracing paper in half to make a piece 24" x 16". Open fold; lightly mark with pencil.

2 Align this fold line with the center back line on collar back pattern. Using an ink pen, trace all the lines. (Dotted lines across the shoulder should be marked with a pencil.)

3 Lift the tracing paper and place the dotted line of the collar back over the corresponding dotted lines of the collar front, matching the notch. Using an ink pen, trace the collar front including the flowers. Erase the pencil lines.

4 Refold the tracing paper and, using an ink pen, trace a second side of the pattern. Label the outside hemlines.

5 Open the pattern, center the fold over the center line of the large flower and, using an ink pen, trace all the lines.

6 Lightly press the pattern

with a warm iron, no steam, to remove center-back fold.

The quilting

1 Place one of the pieces of fabric over the pattern right side up, tape it, and trace all the lines.

2 Place the second piece of fabric on a table wrong side up, smooth the batting over this piece, and then smooth the marked top over the batting; baste.

3 Quilt all the lines except those indicated "outside hemline."

Finishing the collar

1 Cut around the collar ¼" away from the outside hemline.

2 Turn a ¼" hem to the inside on both the lining and top, clipping where necessary on the neck curve, and pin. Blindstitch the folded edges together around the entire outside edge of the collar.

3 Wash the collar by hand, roll it in a towel to remove the water, pull it gently into shape, and dry it flat on a towel.

4 Stuff the flower channels, the channels around the outside edges, and the areas indicated in the pattern with an X, according to the instructions

5 Sew a hook and eye in place to hold the collar closed at the center front (at star marked on pattern).

Variations on the collar

1 For a reversible collar, two different colors of fabric may be used for the back and front of the collar.

2 Other pattern motifs given in this book, such as the butterflies, may be substituted or used with the flowers.

3 Snowflakes cut from folded freezer paper may be bonded directly to the collar top (see pages 19, 49, 50, and 51), quilted around, then removed. This is particularly convenient for dark fabrics, as it eliminates the need for marking.

Projects and Patterns

Reversible Trapunto Purse

Photographs of both purses are on page 28; patterns for the butterfly motifs are on page 45.

Materials

1. Two pieces of white, off-white, or light-colored fabric 30" long by 18" wide. Since the purse will be reversible, the fabrics may be different colors.
2. One piece of batting 30" x 18"
3. Sewing and quilting thread to match
4. Fabric-marking pencil
5. One yard of satin braid for shoulder strap
6. Stuffing yarn and needle
7. An 8½" x 11" piece of tracing paper
8. 14" quilting hoop (optional)
9. Two small buttons

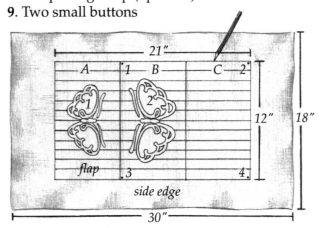

Marking the pattern

1 Draw a rectangle 21" long and 12" wide in the center of one piece of fabric on its right side. With two lines 7" apart, divide the rectangle into three equal segments A, B, and C. Also draw one line through the center lengthwise and a line ¼" inside each end. Mark dots 1, 2, 3, and 4 as shown at left.

2 Fold the tracing paper in half the long way, open it, and lightly mark the fold with pencil. Center this line on the dashed lines of the butterfly patterns and trace each half pattern. Refold the paper and, using a pen, complete each butterfly. Cut the butterflies apart.

3 Center fabric over pattern and trace butterfly 1 in section A and butterfly 2 in section B with their heads facing each other.

4 Using a C-Thru ruler, mark the background quilting lines 1" apart lengthwise from the center line to the edge, stopping these lines ¼" from the ends.

When finished, the piece should look like the diagram at left.

The quilting

Quilt the butterflies and background lines, stopping the background quilting ¼" inside the end lines. Do not quilt the lines marked "side edge."

Constructing the purse

1 Trim away the fabric and batting ¼" outside the rectangle. Trim away an additional ¼" of batting on all four edges.

2 To form the purse pouch, pin the side edges of section C to section B, right sides together, folding on the line and matching dot 1 to dot 2 and dot 3 to dot 4. Fold lining and batting out of the way and machine stitch ¼" from the cut edges, stopping at dots.

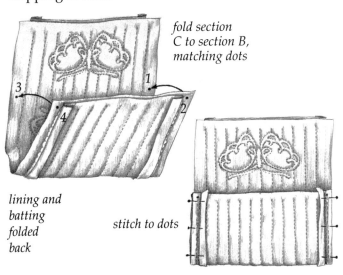

fold section C to section B, matching dots

lining and batting folded back

stitch to dots

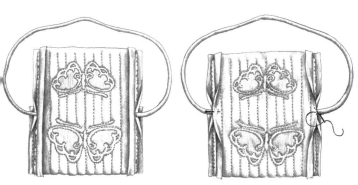

3 Insert the ends of the shoulder strap in the side seams at the ends of the stitching, between the layers. Turn under ¼" on both sides; blindstitch just enough to secure the strap.

4 To finish the top of the pouch, turn under both fabrics ¼" and blind-stitch. Quilt ¼" from edge.

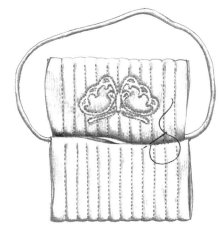

5 For the sides of the pouch, "finger press" the seam allowances and the front lining toward the back of the purse. Turn under ¼" on the back lining, and blindstitch the back lining over the seam and front lining.

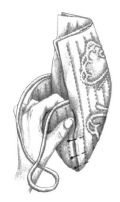

Finishing the purse

1 Turn the purse right side out. Make the button loop: Using some of the leftover fabric cut away from the edge, cut a strip of fabric ¾" wide and 2" long. Turn under ⅛" on each long edge, then fold strip in half lengthwise. Machine stitch as close to the folded edge as possible.

2 Finish the flap edges by turning a ¼" hem to the inside on both the top and lining and blindstitching the folded edges together, catching the loop in the hem. Quilt ¼" from end edge.

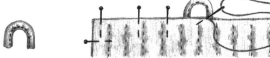

3 Wash and block the purse and dry it on a towel. Working on the inside, stuff the channels and bodies of the butterflies. Sew buttons on the inside and outside of pouch for a reversible purse.

Floral Chintz Purse

Materials

1. A strip of printed floral chintz 30" long and 18" wide, cut from a part of the fabric in which the flowers are centered. (The purse shown on page 28 was made of a lengthwise-stripe chintz fabric with the flowers centered.)
2. A strip of solid fabric that coordinates with the floral chintz, 30" long and 18" wide.
3. One piece of batting 30" x 18"
4. Sewing and quilting thread to match
5. Fabric-marking pencil
6. One yard of braid for shoulder strap
7. Stuffing yarn and needle
8. 14" quilting hoop (optional)
9. Two small buttons

Marking the pattern

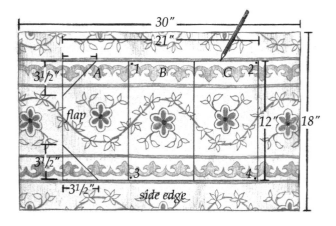

1 Referring to the diagram above and using the fabric-marking pencil, draw a rectangle 21" long and 12" wide, centered on a segment with good-sized flowers. If you are using a striped chintz, let the edge of the stripe dictate the side edge of the rectangle.

2 Draw lines 7" apart, dividing the rectangle into three segments A, B, and C. On segment

A, mark four points, each 3½" from the corners, and draw two lines connecting them as shown on the diagram to form the angles of the flap. Draw a line ¼" inside these lines and the end lines, and a line 1" from the long edge of the rectangle.

3 Mark dots 1, 2, 3, and 4. Note: Because you will be quilting around the printed fabric design, no other pattern lines are necessary.

Quilting the purse

Quilt around the printed fabric design. You do not have to quilt every line, but do quilt enough so that the pattern is attractive on the reverse side of the purse. Stop the quilting at the guidelines ¼" from the ends and 1" from the long sides.

Finishing the purse

1 The Floral Chintz Purse is constructed the same as the Reversible Trapunto Purse in the preceding instructions. After step 5 turn the purse right side out.

2 Finish the flap edges by turning a ¼" hem to the inside on both the top and the lining and blindstitching the folded edges together.

3 Add a line of quilting ¼" from the finished edges of the flap.

4 Make a buttonhole in the flap and sew buttons to both the inside and outside of the purse (to make it reversible).

5 Wash and block the purse to shape and dry it flat on a towel.

6 Working on the inside of the purse, stuff the areas that have been created by the quilting according to the general instructions.

Trapunto Belt

Photo is on page 27; pattern is on page 45.

Materials

1. Two strips of fabric 8" wide and 6" longer than your waist size
2. One piece of batting 8" x 20"
3. ½ yard of lightweight fusible interfacing
4. Sewing and quilting thread to match
5. Fabric-marking pencil and black felt-tip pen
6. 2" of Velcro™

Marking the pattern

1 Center fabric over the pattern and trace all the lines. Lift the fabric, turn, match the center line, and trace the second side. Mark the dots.

2 With a ruler, extend the lines from both ends of the pattern so that the total length of the belt is 4½" longer than your waist size.

3 Bond a piece of lightweight fusible interfacing on the back of each extension and center a 20"-long piece of batting or flannel on the front design section.

Quilting the belt

1 Layer the top (with batting) and back; baste the layers.

2 Quilt the design, stopping at the circles and leaving thread to finish the quilting after hemming. Quilt the lines ½" from the hemline on the extension.

Constructing the belt

1 Cut ¼" outside the hemline, turn a ¼" hem to the inside on both the top and back, and blindstitch the folded edges together. Finish the quilting with the leftover thread. Wash and block the belt.

2 Stuff the center areas from the back, according to the general directions.

3 Try on the belt, allowing the ends to overlap comfortably. Mark overlap with pin; sew Velcro in place.

Optional freezer-paper method for dark fabrics

For dark fabric, the design motif can be cut from freezer paper and temporarily bonded to the fabric while the design is quilted.

To use this method for the belt, cut a piece of freezer paper 22" x 10". Fold paper in half crosswise; crease to mark center. Unfold paper and place it over pattern on page 45 with crease on center line. Trace the half pattern, including dotted lines where indicated. Mark dots. Refold pattern; staple along edges and down center to hold layers. Cut out pattern. The shaded areas will fall away. Remove staples and open pattern.

Fold fabric in half crosswise to find center; unfold. Place pattern shiny side down on right side of fabric with centers matched. Working on a hard surface covered with a dish towel, bond the pattern in place by pressing (without steam).

With a light marking pencil, extend the lines from both ends of the pattern so that the total length is 4½" longer than your waist size.

As explained above, bond the interfacing, layer and baste the top (with batting) and back, and quilt the belt. When quilting, use the point of the needle to tear the freezer-paper pattern at the places indicated with dotted lines so that you can quilt in those areas.

Ruffled Trellis Pillow

A photo of the pillow is on page 25.

Materials

1. Two 24" squares of white, off-white, or light-colored fabric, plus ½ yard more for the ruffle. (Note: If your fabric is narrower than 40", get ⅔ yard extra for ruffle.)
2. 1¾ yards of pre-gathered lace ½" to ¾" wide.
3. One 24" square of muslin
4. One 24" square of batting
5. Quilting and sewing thread to match fabric
6. 14" of ¾"-wide white Velcro™
7. Fabric-marking pencil and a black felt-tip pen
8. Stuffing yarn and stuffing needle
9. 24" square piece of tracing paper for pattern
10. One firm 14" knife-edge pillow form
11. One 14" or 12" quilting hoop (optional)

Preparing the pattern

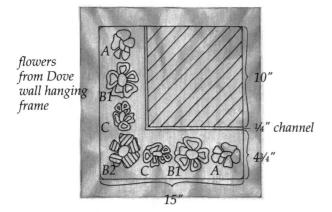

flowers from Dove wall hanging frame

1 Lay the tracing paper out on a table and, using a clear plastic ruler, draw a 15" square for the outside edge of the pillow. Measuring from one corner, draw two lines to make a 10¼" square, and draw two more lines inside this square to make a 10" square. These lines create a ¼" channel. In the smaller square, draw parallel diagonal lines 1" apart. Using a large spool, curve off each corner, as it is easier to apply the lace and ruffle around a curve.

2 Using a black pen, ink all of these lines.

3 Place the pillow pattern over the frame of the Dove pattern on page 39 so that flowers A, B1, and C fill the border area. Trace these three flowers with the black ink pen. Repeat for the second side.

4 Center the corner of the pillow pattern over flower B2 (page 39) and trace it with the pen. The completed pattern should look like the diagram at left.

Making the pillow top

1 Center one of the 24" squares of fabric over the pattern right side up, and trace all the lines onto the fabric.

2 Place the 24" square of muslin on a table and layer the batting and marked pillow top over it. Baste.

3 Quilt all the lines except those on the outer edge.

4 Baste through the lines of the 15" curved-corner square to mark the outside edge of the pillow.

Making the ruffle

1 Cut three 5½"-wide crosswise strips from the ½ yard extra fabric. (Cut four strips if your fabric is narrower than 40".)

2 Machine stitch these together to make one long strip 5½" wide by at least 120" long. (The length of the ruffle should be at least double the outside measurement of the pillow.) Press the seam allowances open. Turn and stitch a ¼" hem

on each short end of the ruffle.

3 Fold this long strip in half lengthwise, wrong sides together, so that you have a 2¾"-wide strip. Press. Pin along the open edge.

4 Using the longest stitch setting on your machine, make two lines of stitching, one ¼" and one ⅛" from the raw edge of the strip. Pull the threads and gather the strip until it is 60" long.

Applying the lace and ruffle

1 Cut ⅜" outside the basted line that marks the outside edge of the quilted pillow top.

2 Cut a piece of lace 60½" long. Roll a ¼" hem on each short end and hand stitch to prevent raveling.

3 Beginning in the center of one edge, pin the lace to the right side of the pillow top along the basted line that marks the outside edge, placing the free edge of the lace toward the center of the pillow. (See diagram below.) Baste.

 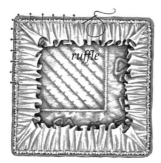

⅜" seam
allowance

4 Starting in the center of the same edge, pin the ruffle to the pillow top over the lace, easing it around the curved corners with the ruffled edge toward the center. (See diagram above.) Use the gathering stitches as a line to match with the basted edge of the lace. Baste the ruffle to the top.

Constructing the pillow back

1 Cut the second 24" square of fabric in half. Press under a 1" hem on one long edge of each half.

2 Separate the Velcro. Pin and machine stitch one part to each half of the pillow back, over the folded hem. The Velcro should go on the right side of one half and the wrong side of the other half (as shown below) so that when rejoined, the pillow back is complete.

3 Rejoin the Velcro and topstitch as indicated below.

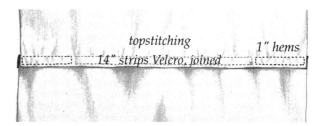

Finishing and stuffing the pillow

1 Placing right sides together, center the pillow top over the pillow back. Make sure that the ruffle is smoothed away from the stitching line. Pin.

2 With the wrong side of pillow top facing up and using the basting as a guide, stitch the top and back together.

3 Trim away excess fabric from the pillow back. Open the Velcro and turn the pillow cover right side out, gently pulling on the ruffle. Rejoin the Velcro.

4 Hand wash the pillow cover, roll it in a towel to remove the water, and block to shape by gently pulling on the outside edges. Dry flat on a

towel or on a clothesline.

ed on pattern with an X.

5 Open the Velcro, turn the pillow cover inside out, and stuff the channels and areas indicat-

6 Turn the pillow cover right side out, and insert the pillow form.

Designs and Borders for a Large Quilt

Interlocking Squares border

This border pattern (half motif given on the next page) is wonderful because it is actually so much less complex than it looks, and it may be adapted for many border sizes. The only requirement is that the width of the border (8") must divide evenly into the length of the border so that the squares will meet exactly in the corner. It works easily for a square quilt such as one for a king-size bed, but it can also be used for a rectangular format as long as the two dimensions are both multiples of eight.

The "Square Dance" quilt required a border 80" long. A square that is 8" across repeats 10 times along each side, with an additional square in each corner to meet the

Interlocking Squares Border Unit

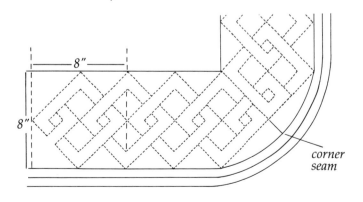

corner seam

adjoining pattern at the mitered-corner seam. Two 1" channels were added on the outside edge to bring the total border width to 10". Study the diagram below left to see how the squares in this border are overlapped and intertwined.

"Homage" feather border

The feather border (pattern given on page 46) from the quilt "Homage" can be adapted to fit any length and for widths from 8½" to 12". It looks best in a space 10" wide. To adapt this border for your quilt:

1 Fold an 8" x 10" piece of tracing paper in half crosswise; unfold. Match fold line to dotted line of Unit A and use an ink pen to trace half motif. Refold paper and mark the other half. Use another piece of paper and trace Unit B. Tape these patterns to a table.

2 Find and mark the center of the border fabric both crosswise and lengthwise by folding and finger pressing or by measuring and marking. Center the fabric over Unit A pattern and use a pencil to trace motif, omitting the end "knob." Mark the two diamonds.

3 Move fabric to pattern for Unit B and match marked diamonds with pattern diamonds. Trace the six feathers in Unit B. Move fabric, matching diamonds with pattern squares, and trace Unit B again.

4 Continue tracing feathers until border is the correct length. Finally, position border fabric over Unit A pattern, matching marked squares with pattern diamonds, and trace end "knob."

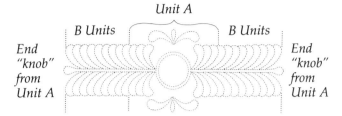

Unit A

B Units   B Units

End "knob" from Unit A   End "knob" from Unit A

5 Working in the opposite direction from the center motif, repeat these steps to complete the entire border. The border should look like the diagram at the left, varying in length to fit your quilt.

The additional feather motifs given on page 47 and below coordinate with the feather border. The Square Feather design below will fit a 10" block and could be used to alternate with pieced or appliquéd blocks. The remaining Triangle Feather design (page 47) will fit in a half block with a 10" side and can be used to finish the edge of a quilt with blocks set on point.

Interlocking Squares border

center

To make complete pattern, fold a 9" square of tracing paper in half crosswise. Unfold and match crease to center line. Trace half motif; rotate paper and trace again.

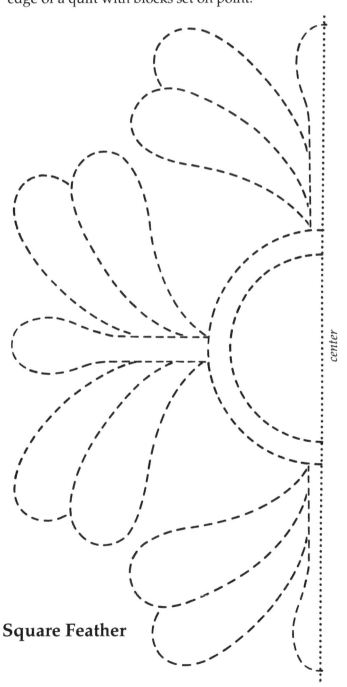

center

Square Feather

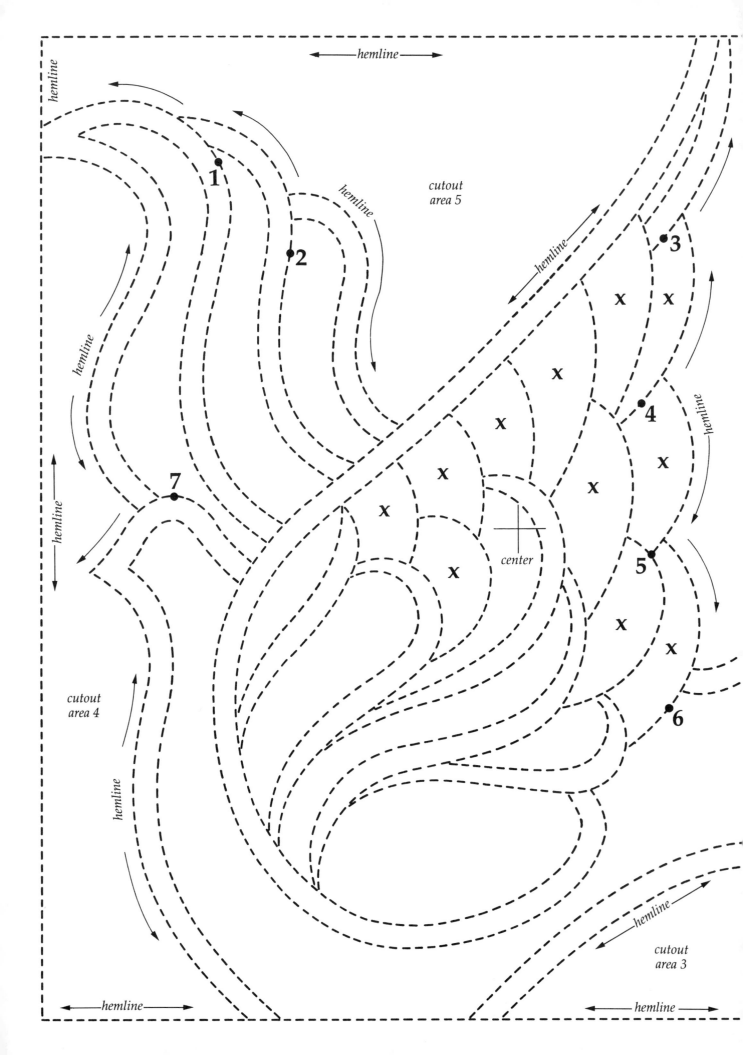

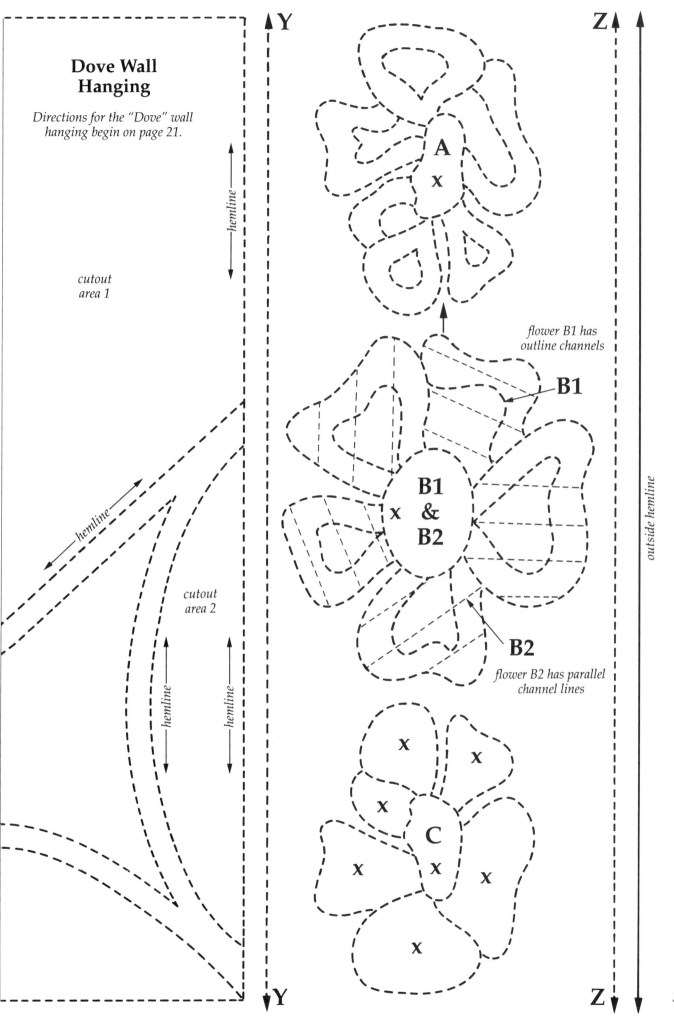

Dove Wall Hanging

Directions for the "Dove" wall hanging begin on page 21.

cutout area 1

hemline

hemline

cutout area 2

hemline

hemline

Y

Y

Z

Z

A

x

flower B1 has outline channels

B1

B1 & B2

x

B2

flower B2 has parallel channel lines

outside hemline

C

x

x

x

x

x

x

x

Large Flower for Vest
Directions for the vest begin on page 23.

top

center

center

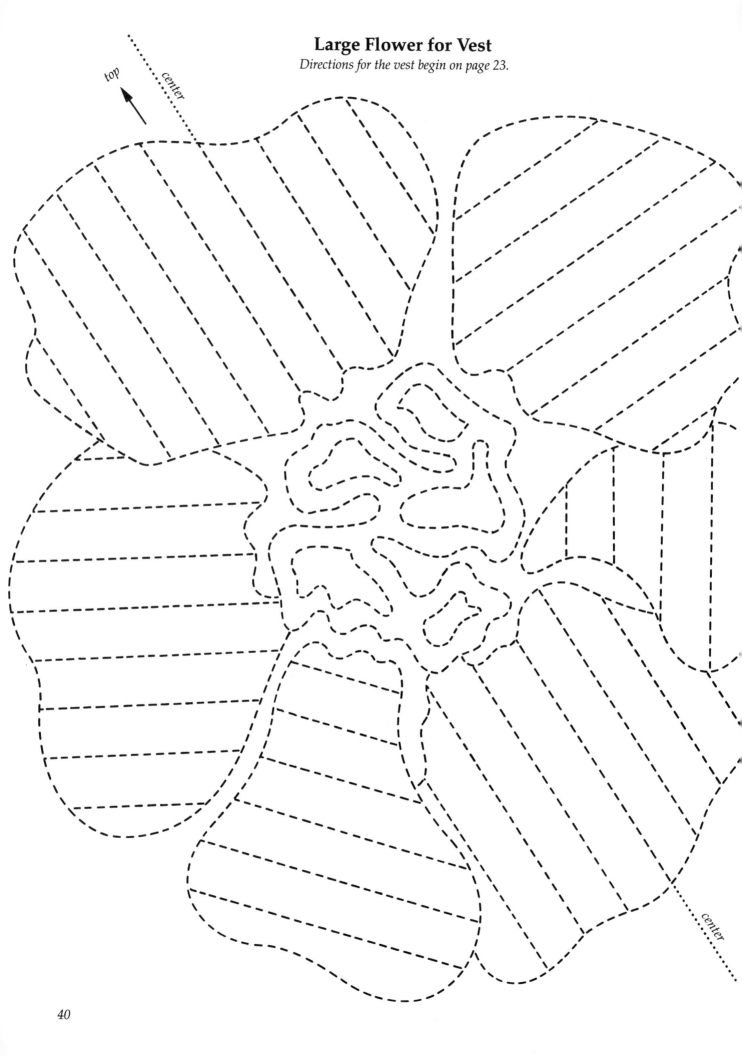

Small Flowers for Vest

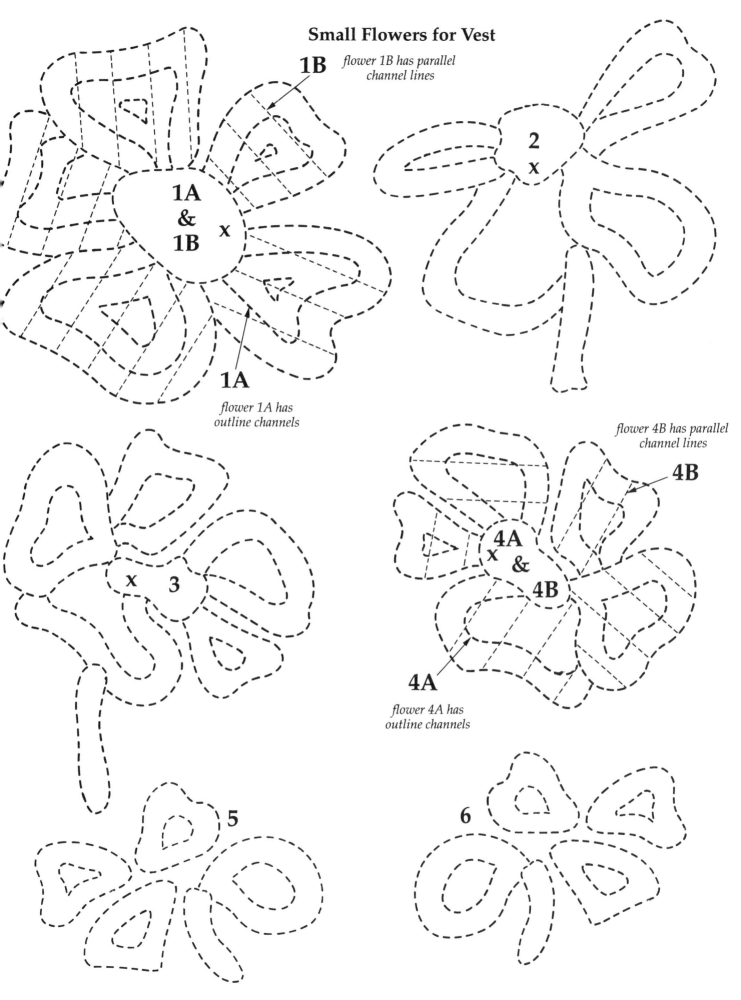

1B *flower 1B has parallel channel lines*

1A & 1B x

1A *flower 1A has outline channels*

2 x

x **3**

4B *flower 4B has parallel channel lines*

4A & 4B x

4A *flower 4A has outline channels*

5

6

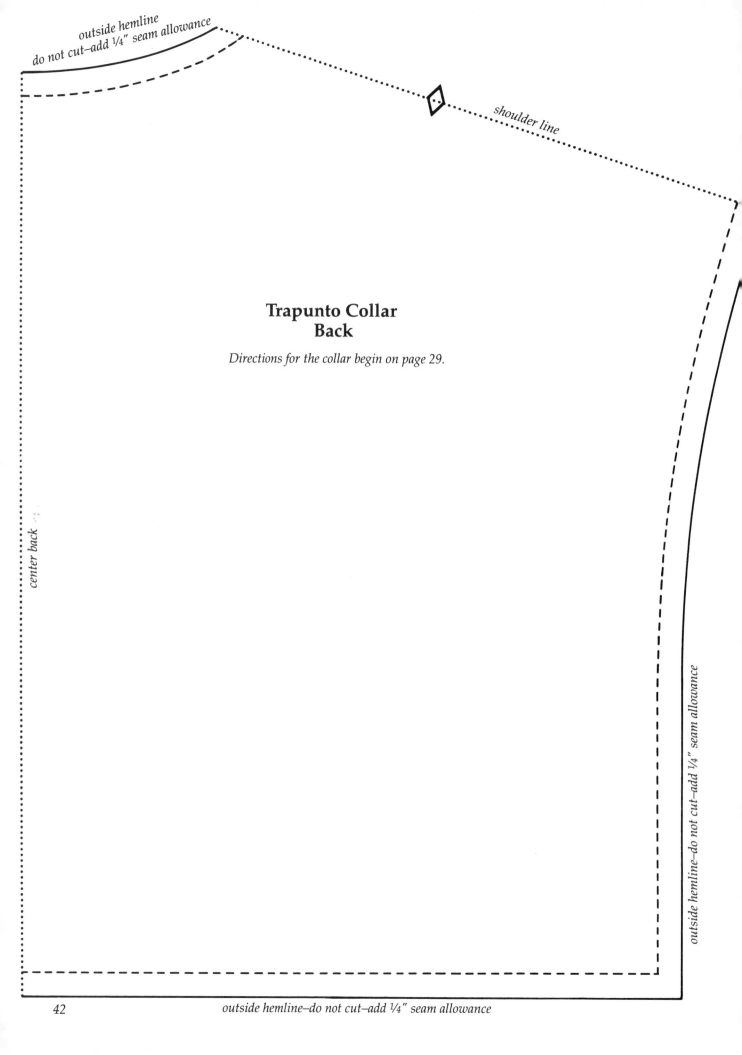

outside hemline
do not cut–add ¼" seam allowance

shoulder line

Trapunto Collar
Back

Directions for the collar begin on page 29.

center back

outside hemline–do not cut–add ¼" seam allowance

outside hemline–do not cut–add ¼" seam allowance

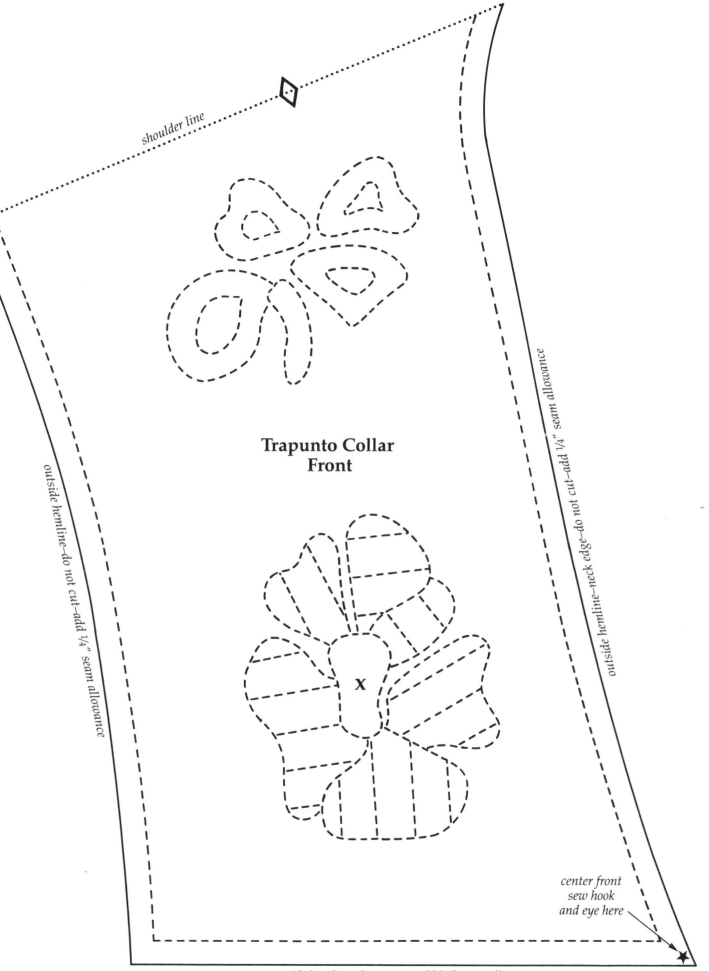

shoulder line

Trapunto Collar Front

X

outside hemline–do not cut–add ¼" seam allowance

outside hemline–neck edge–do not cut–add ¼" seam allowance

center front
sew hook
and eye here

outside hemline–do not cut–add ¼" seam allowance

Large Flower for Collar

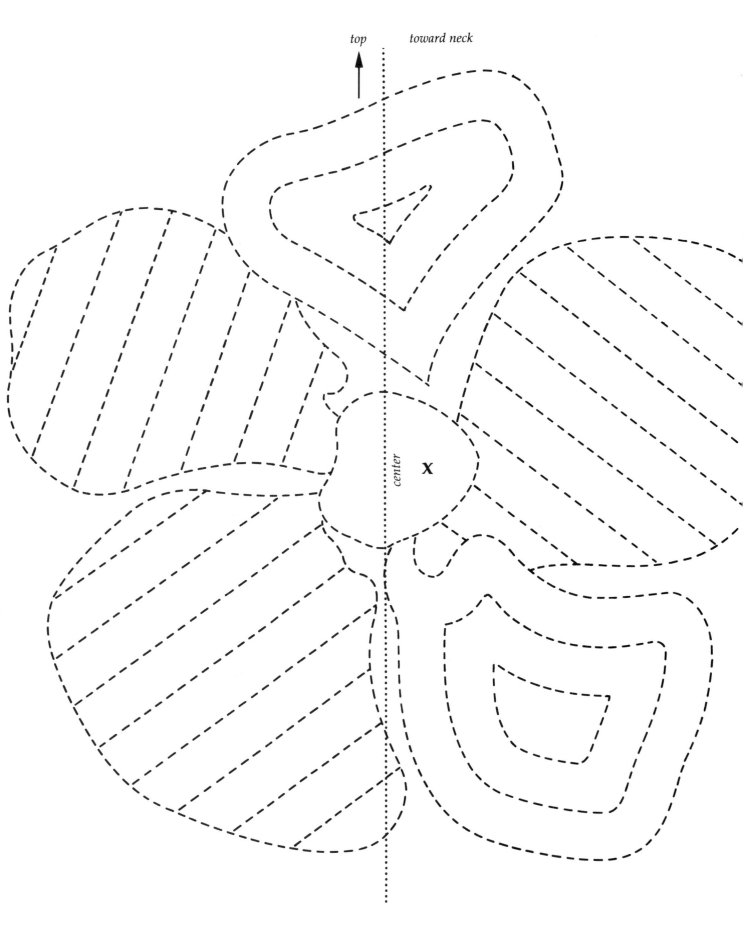

top   *toward neck*

center

X

Trapunto Belt

Directions for the belt are on page 33.

Butterflies for Reversible Trapunto Purse

Directions for the reversible purse begin on page 30.

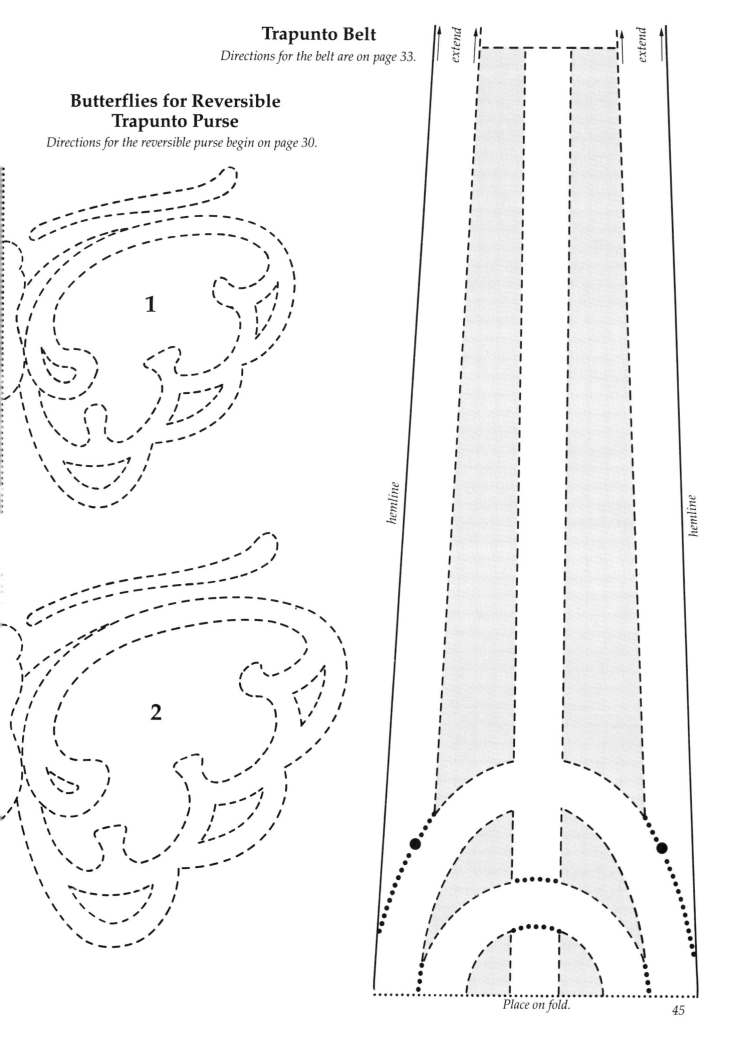

1

2

extend

extend

hemline

hemline

Place on fold.

"Homage" Feather Border

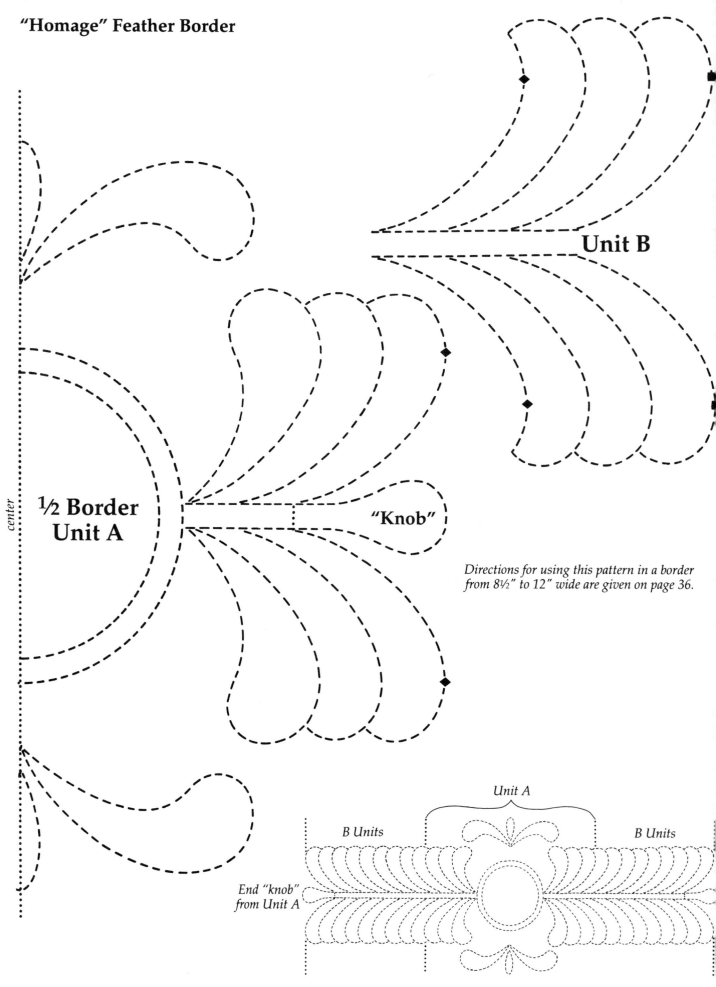

Unit B

½ Border Unit A

center

"Knob"

Directions for using this pattern in a border from 8½" to 12" wide are given on page 36.

Unit A

B Units

B Units

End "knob" from Unit A

46

The drawing below shows how Triangle Feather, at right, and Feather Border, Square Feather, and Flower Motifs on pages 37, 39, 40, 41, 43, 44, and 46 can be used in a small lap quilt, a child's quilt, or in an elegant throw for the back of a couch or chair. The Flower Motifs can be scattered as desired over the middle portion of the quilt, then channels of trapunto, either straight or curved as you wish, can be added to connect the motifs.

Triangle Feather

More uses for flowers and butterflies

In the previous projects, patterns for 16 flowers and two butterflies have been given. These motifs coordinate very well and could be used in many ways. The large flowers could be repeated around the bottom of a skirt, or they could be arranged in combination with butterflies across a skirt. Any of these motifs could be used on a pillow, on the top of a fabric-covered box, or on a tote bag. The large flowers could be used in plain blocks, with some of the small ones repeated in a quilt border. This arrangement would be particularly charming on a floral appliqué crib quilt. As I have suggested before, photocopy the motifs and play with them on your project. The possibilities for these and other simple designs are endless, and as you use them you will begin to understand how to create designs of your own.

Four snowflakes and ways to use them

These four snowflakes were selected from the 24 on the quilt "Blizzard of '83." Two are 8", one is 10", and one is 12" in diameter. These motifs will fit in blocks 10", 12", and 14" respectively. They can be used on clothing, tote bags, or on pillow tops. To make a pattern, trace the half pattern onto folded tracing paper, then trace a second half to complete the entire pattern. This whole pattern can now be transferred to fabric.

The half patterns given can be used also in borders or in half squares as shown below.

Half Block

Border 1

Border 2

center

10" Snowflake

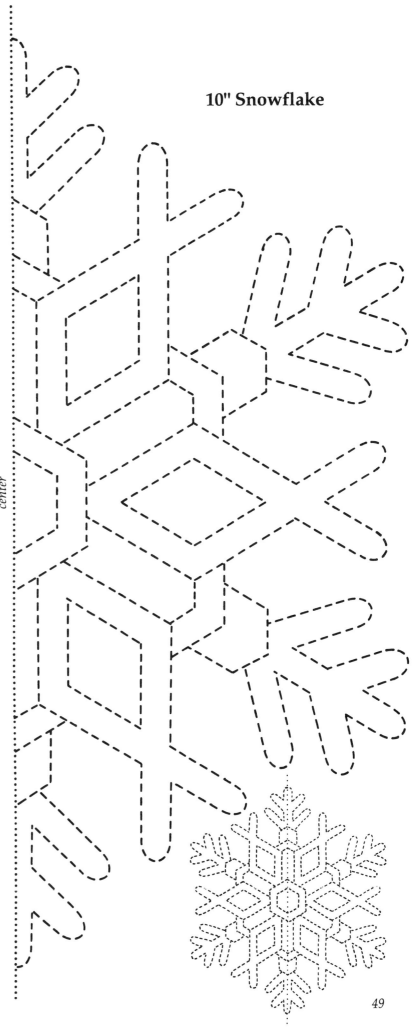

8" Snowflake

8" Snowflake

center

12" Snowflake

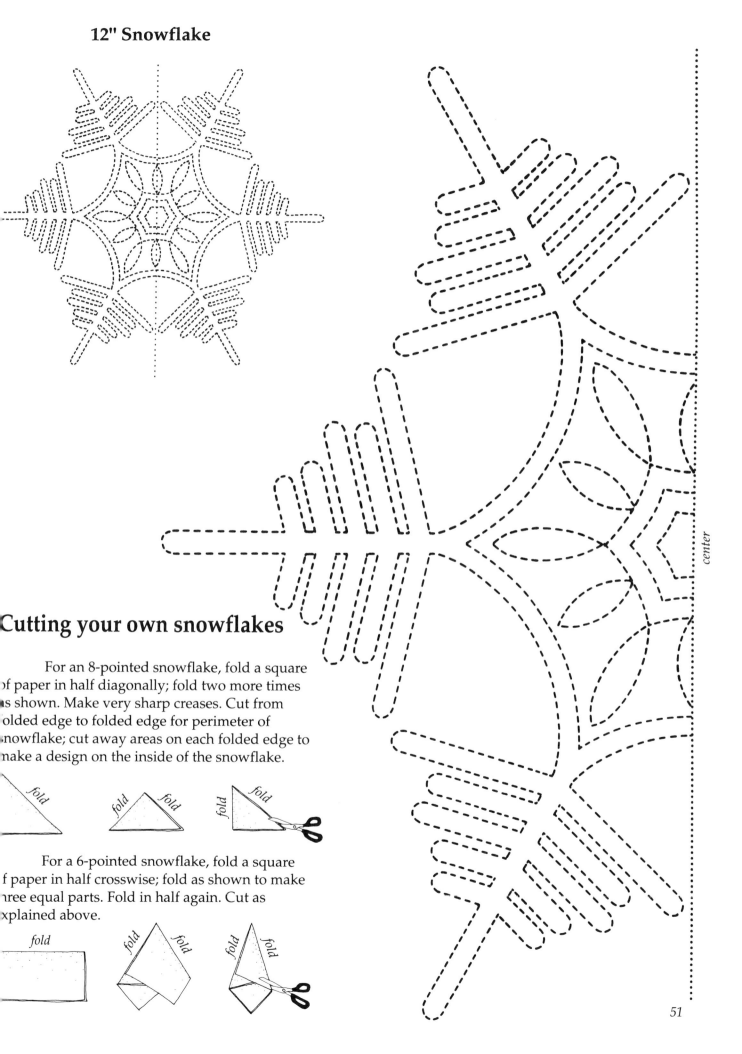

center

Cutting your own snowflakes

For an 8-pointed snowflake, fold a square of paper in half diagonally; fold two more times as shown. Make very sharp creases. Cut from folded edge to folded edge for perimeter of snowflake; cut away areas on each folded edge to make a design on the inside of the snowflake.

fold *fold* *fold* *fold* *fold*

For a 6-pointed snowflake, fold a square of paper in half crosswise; fold as shown to make three equal parts. Fold in half again. Cut as explained above.

fold *fold* *fold* *fold* *fold*

Bibliography

Bodger, Lorraine. *Paper Dreams*. New York: Universe Press, 1977.

Inglis, Charlotte. *Making Your Own Custom Quilting Stencils Using the "Snowflake" Method*. Dexter, Michigan: Inglis Publications, 1981.

Johnson, Pauline. *Creating With Paper, Basic Forms and Variations*. Seattle, Washington: University of Washington Press, 1958.

Morgan, Mary and Dee Mosteller. *Trapunto and Other Forms of Raised Quilting*. New York: Charles Scribner's Sons, 1977.

Orlofsky, Patsy and Myron Orlofsky. *Quilts in America*. New York: McGraw-Hill Book Company, 1974.

Reed, Brenda Lee. *Easy To Make Decorative Paper Snowflakes*. New York: Dover Publications, 1987.

Safford, Carleton L., and Robert Bishop. *America's Quilts and Coverlets*. New York: E. P. Dutton and Co., 1972.

Silvey, Linda, and Loretta Taylor. *Paper and Scissors Polygons*. Sunnyvale, California: Creative Publications, 1976.

▲   ▲   ▲

About the Author

A native of St. Louis, Sue Rodgers taught herself to quilt by making crib quilts for her children in the 1960s. Love of hand quilting led her to trapunto, and her work in this style has been published extensively and has won numerous awards. Her quilt "Shalom" placed second in Quilts: Visions of the World, the first international quilt competition held in Salzburg, Austria, in 1988. Sue teaches trapunto, appliqué, and hand quilting, and she sells her work through exhibitions and on commission. Her quilts are in private collections and that of the Port Authority at the World Trade Center. Her home is in Mountain Lakes, New Jersey.

▲   ▲   ▲

OTHER BOOKS FROM MOON OVER THE MOUNTAIN PUBLISHING COMPANY:

Quick & Cuddly Quilts for Baby
Quilt Settings–A Workbook
Handy-Crafts for Quilt Lovers–Papercrafting with Quilt Art
Scrap Quilts
The Rainbow Collection–Quilt Patterns for Rainbow Colors
Shining Star Quilts
Log Cabin Quilts
Taking the Math Out of Making Patchwork Quilts
How To Make a Quilt–25 Easy Lessons for Beginners
First Aid for Family Quilts
Patchwork Sampler Legacy Quilt (in association with *Quilter's Newsletter Magazine*)

For information on how you can have *Quilter's Newsletter Magazine* delivered to your door, write to: Leman Publications, Inc., 6700 West 44th Avenue, Wheatridge, Colorado 80033.